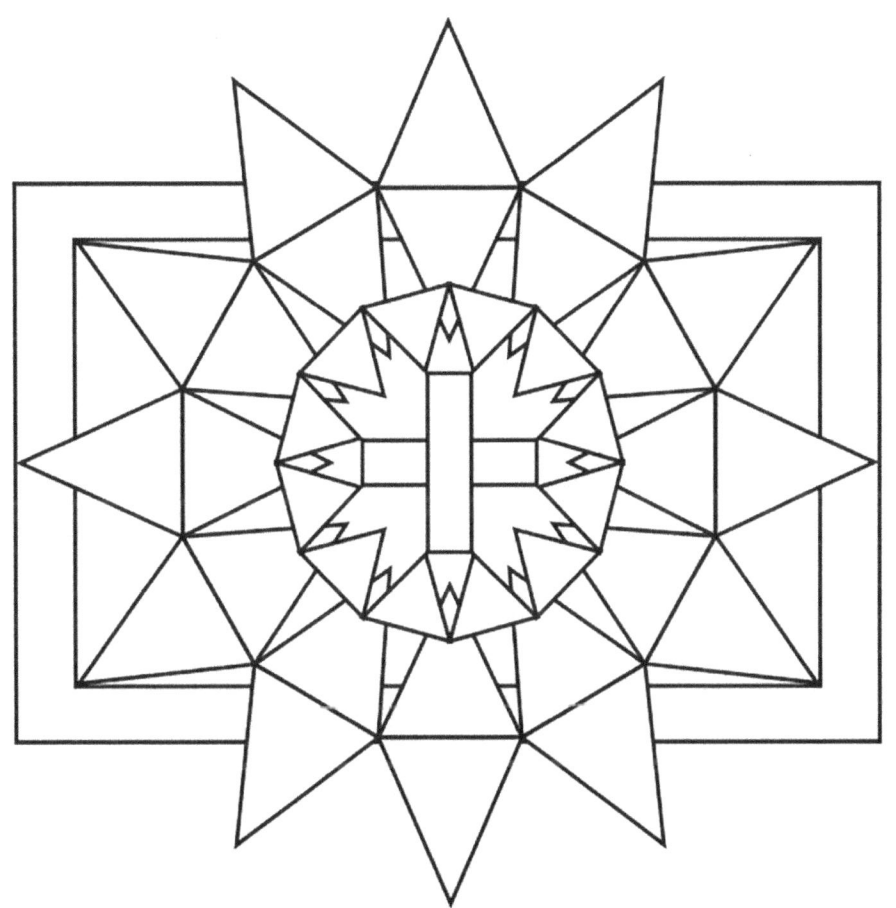

Another Coloring for Autistic Children and Adults

Like my first book, Coloring Book for Autistic Children and Adults, you might want to put a blank piece of paper or thin cardboard behind the design before you begin to color. This will catch any colors that bleed through.

There are many mediums you can use to color. I suggest using markers, colored pencils, gel pens, or watercolor pencils.

Have fun!

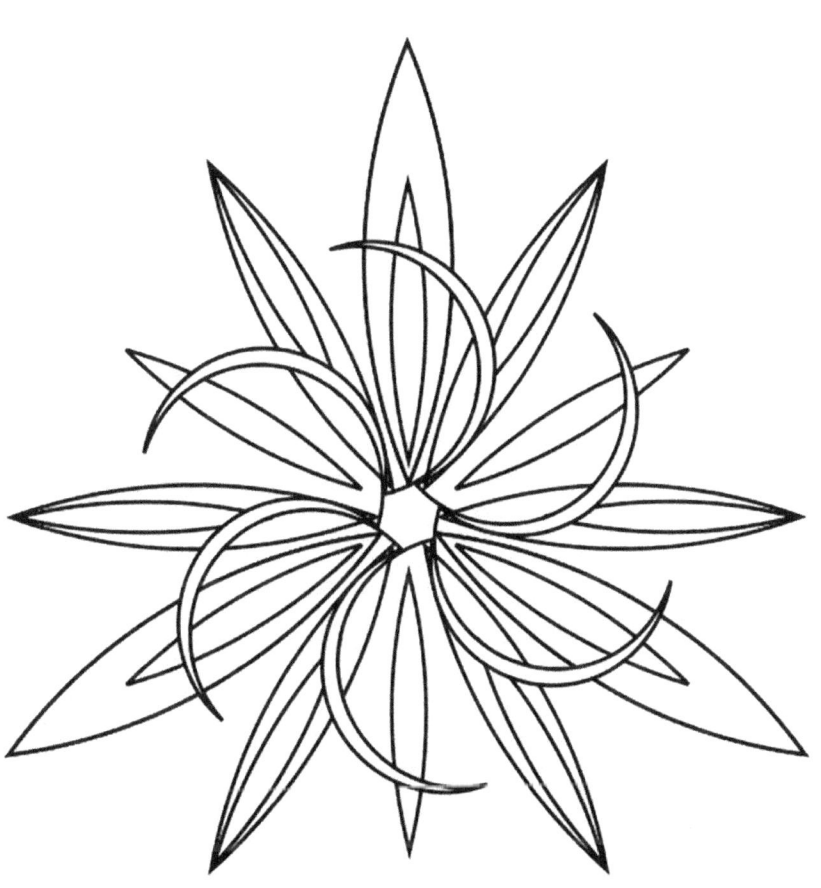

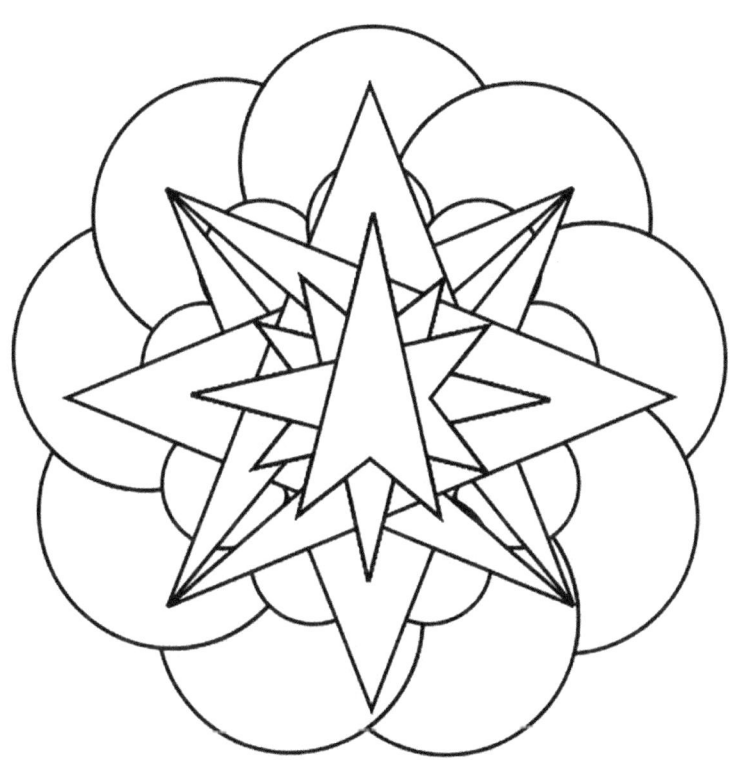

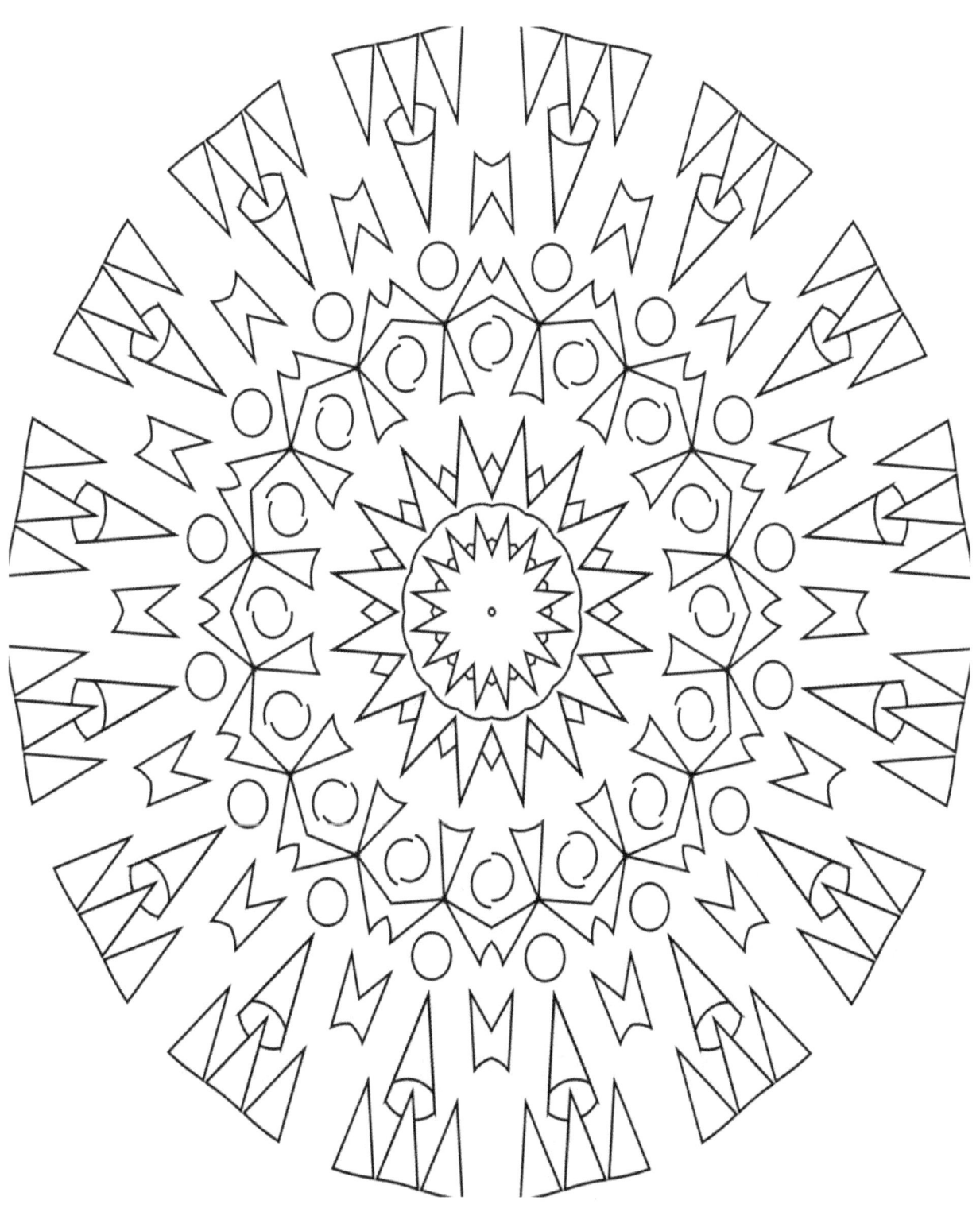

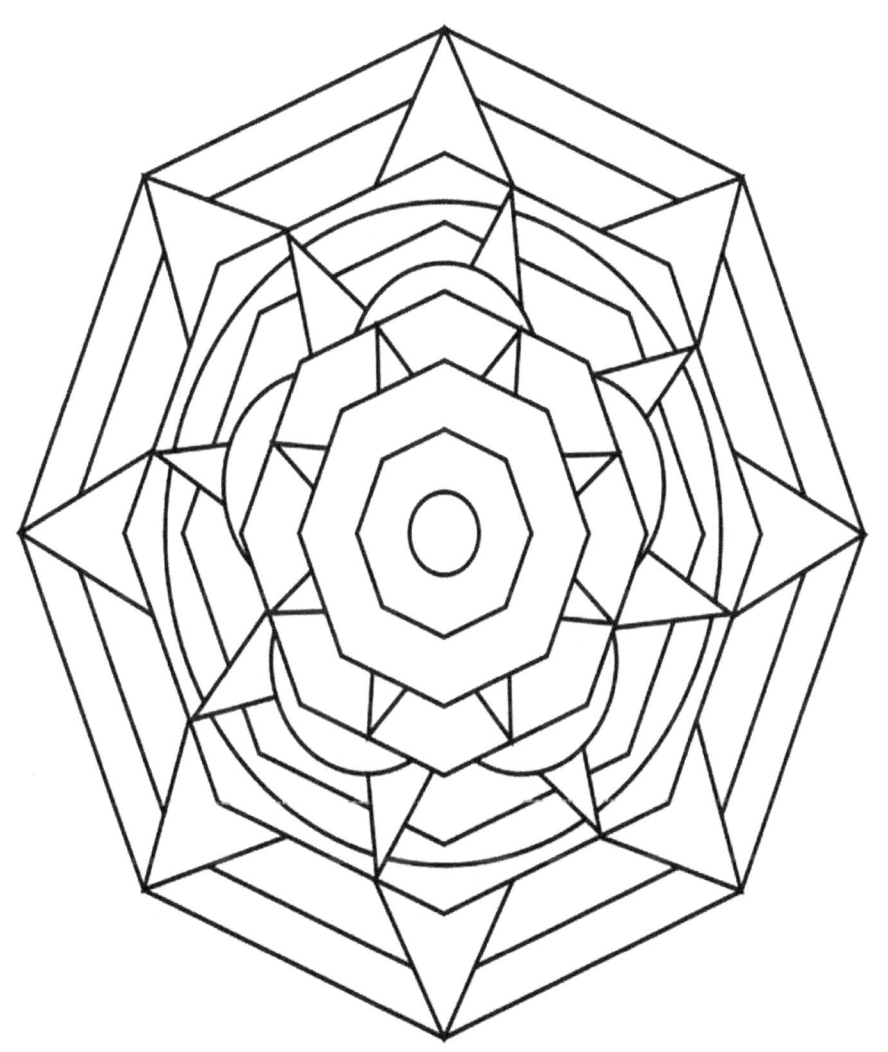

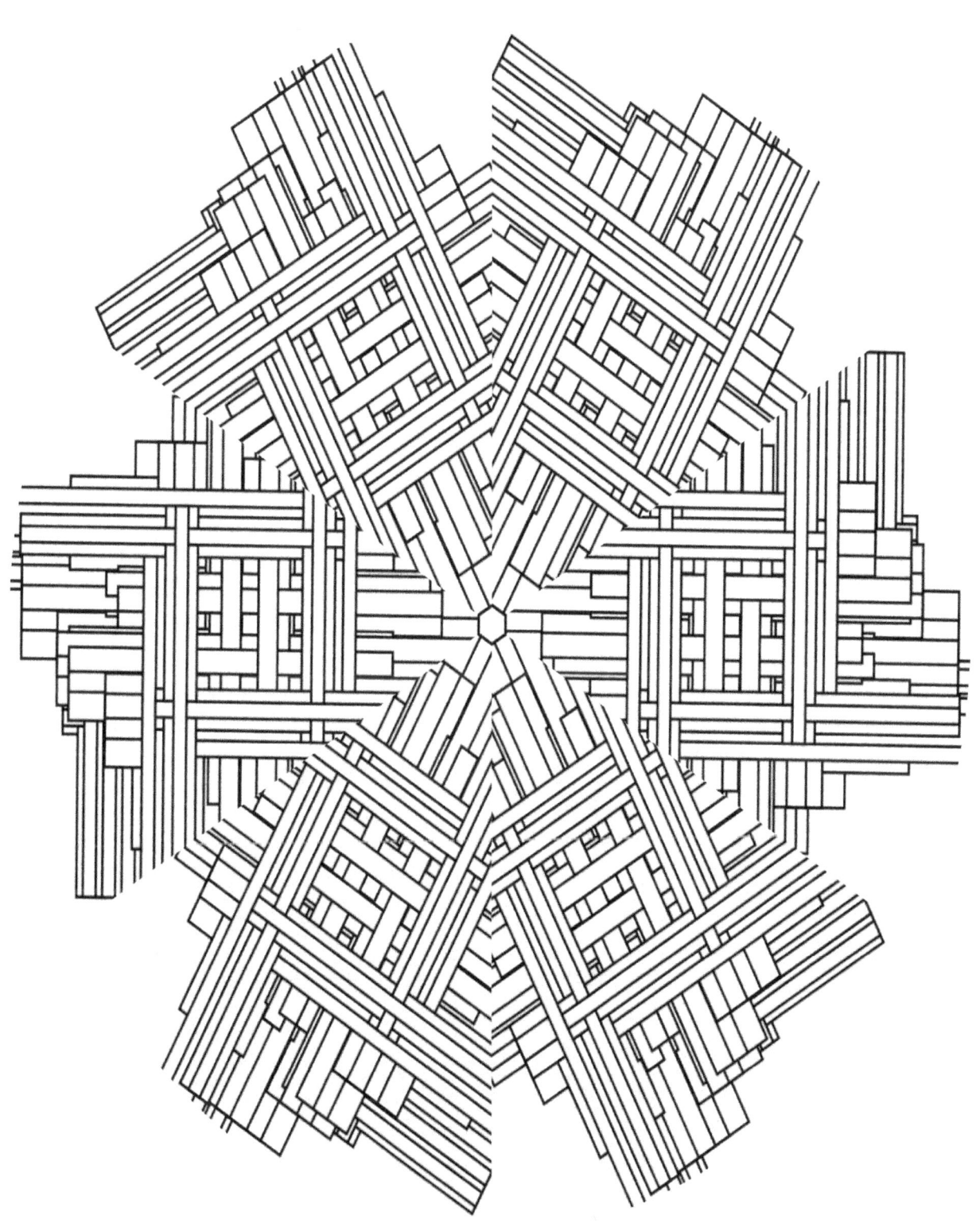

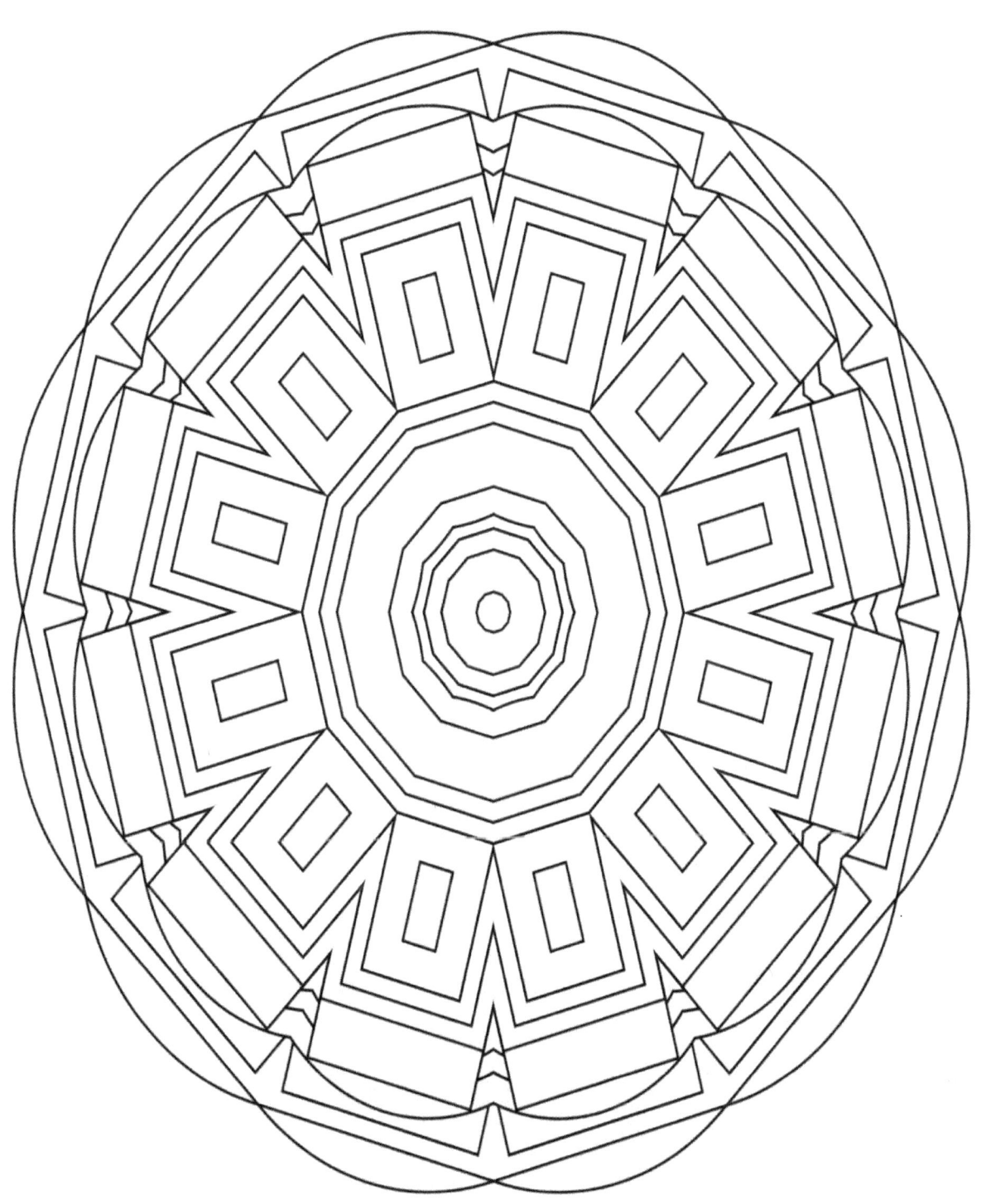

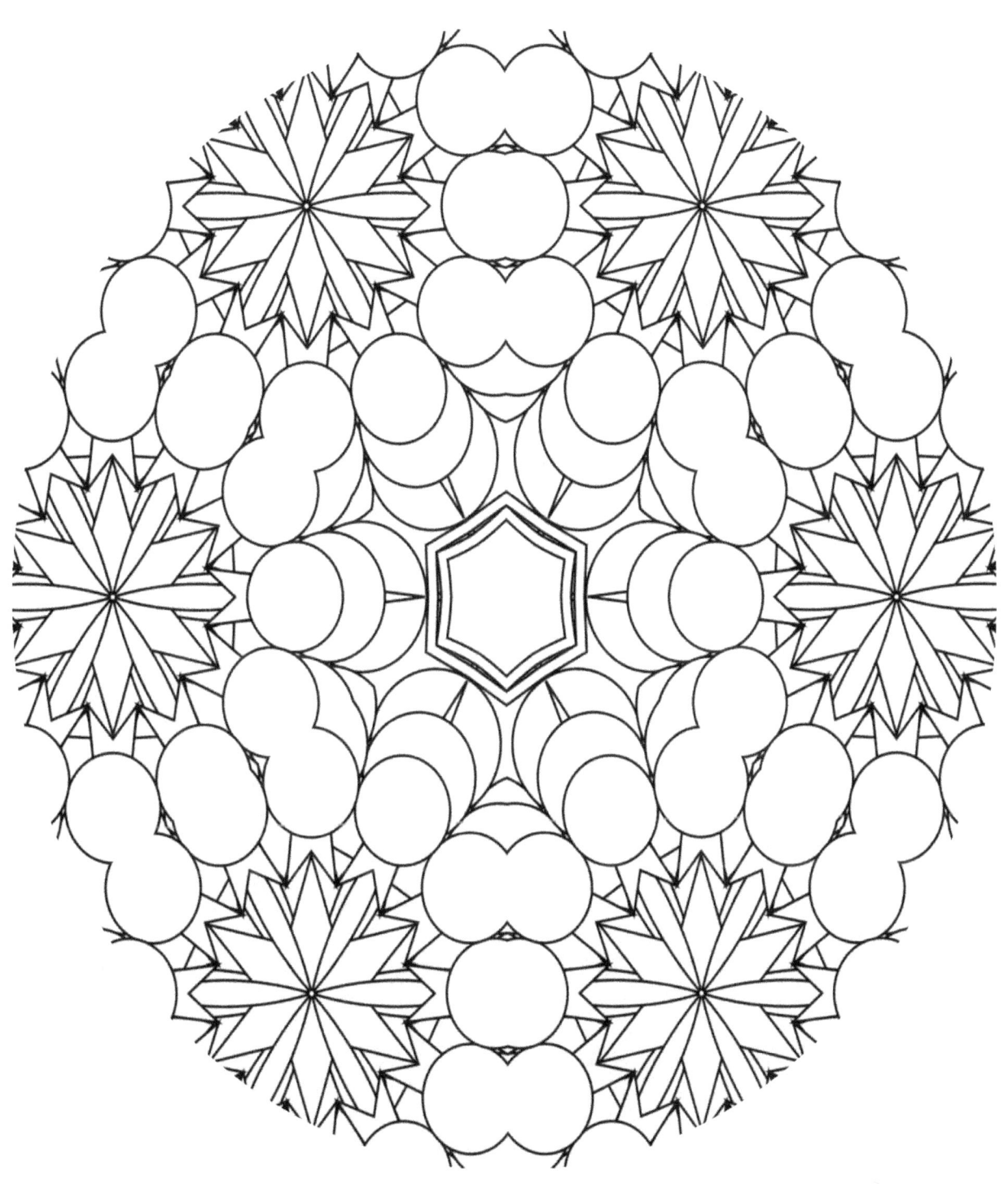

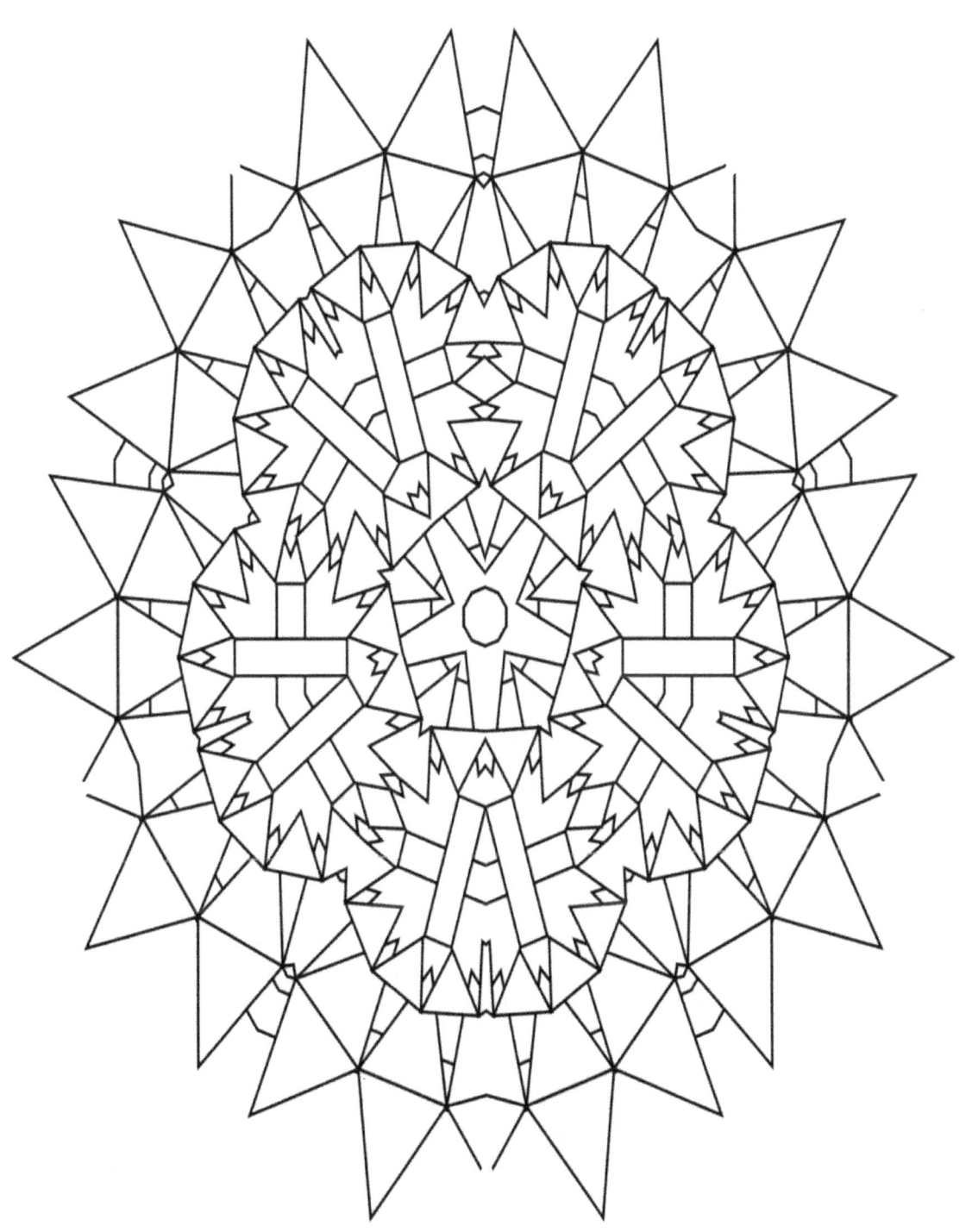

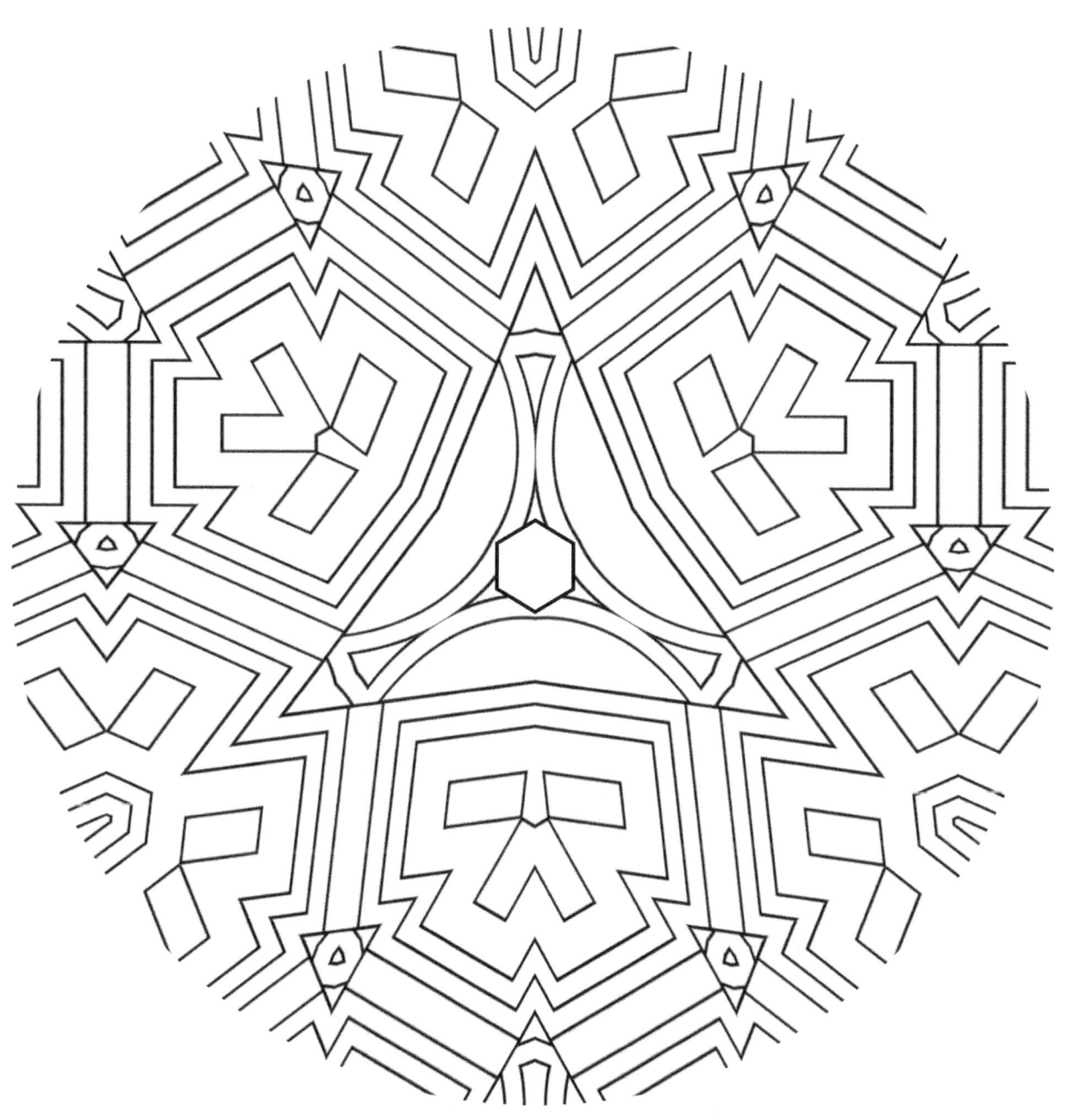

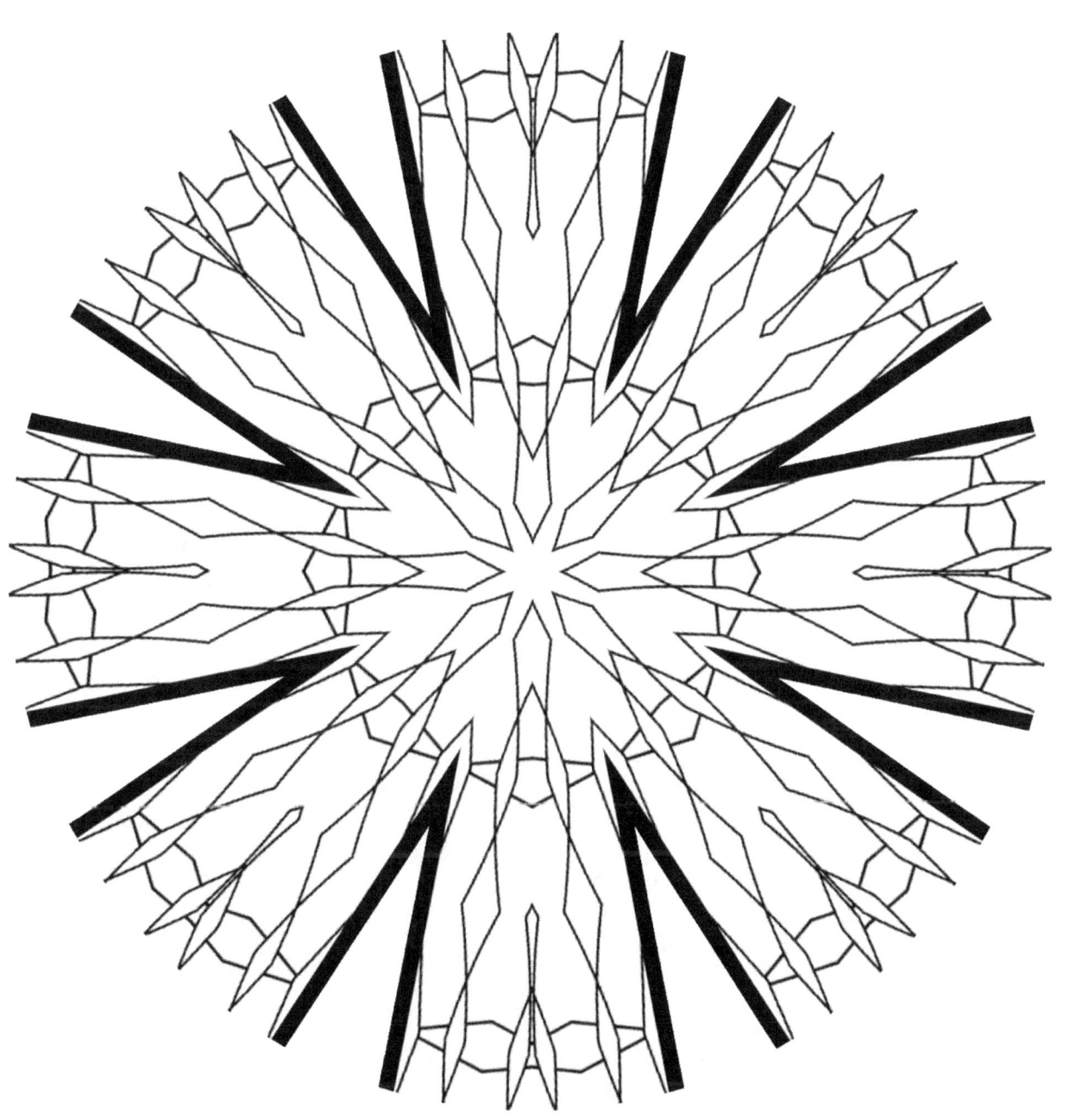

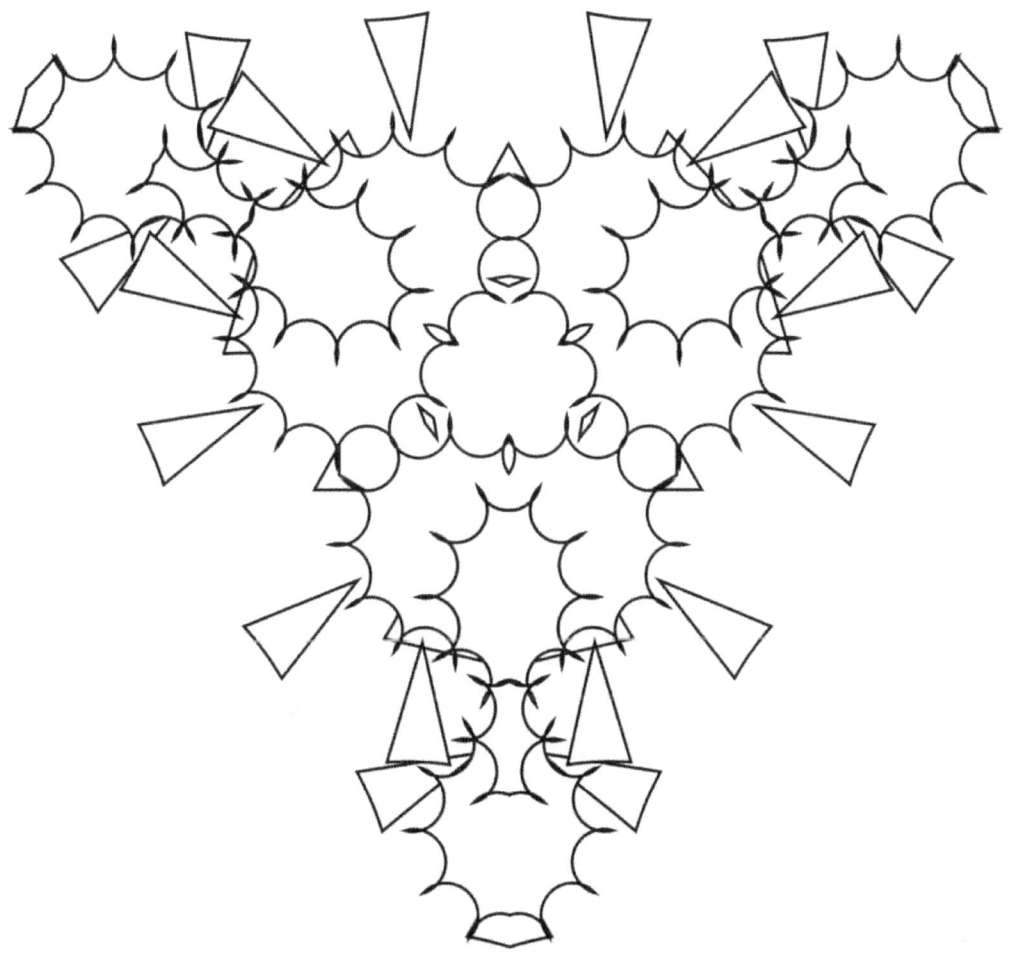

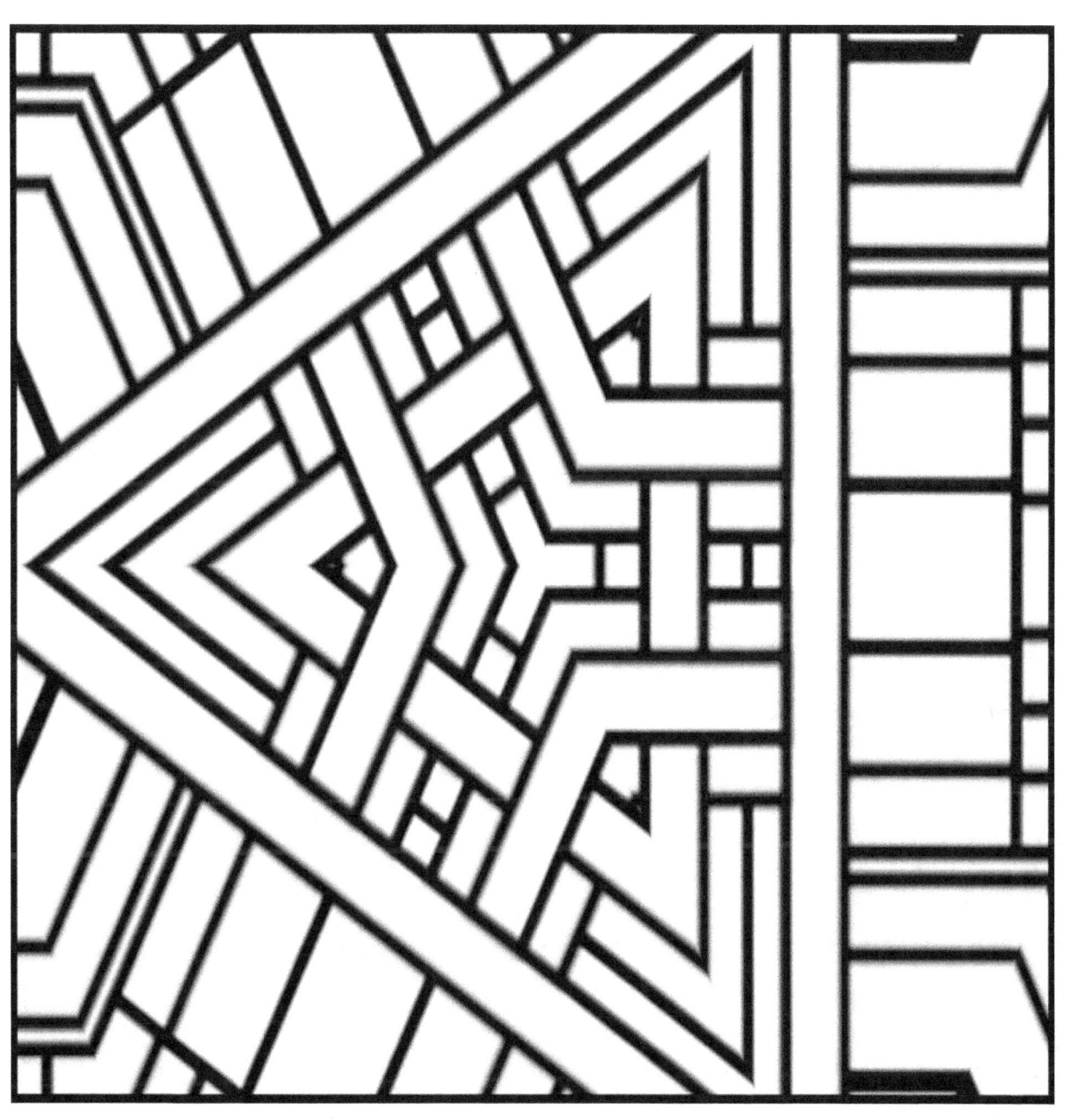

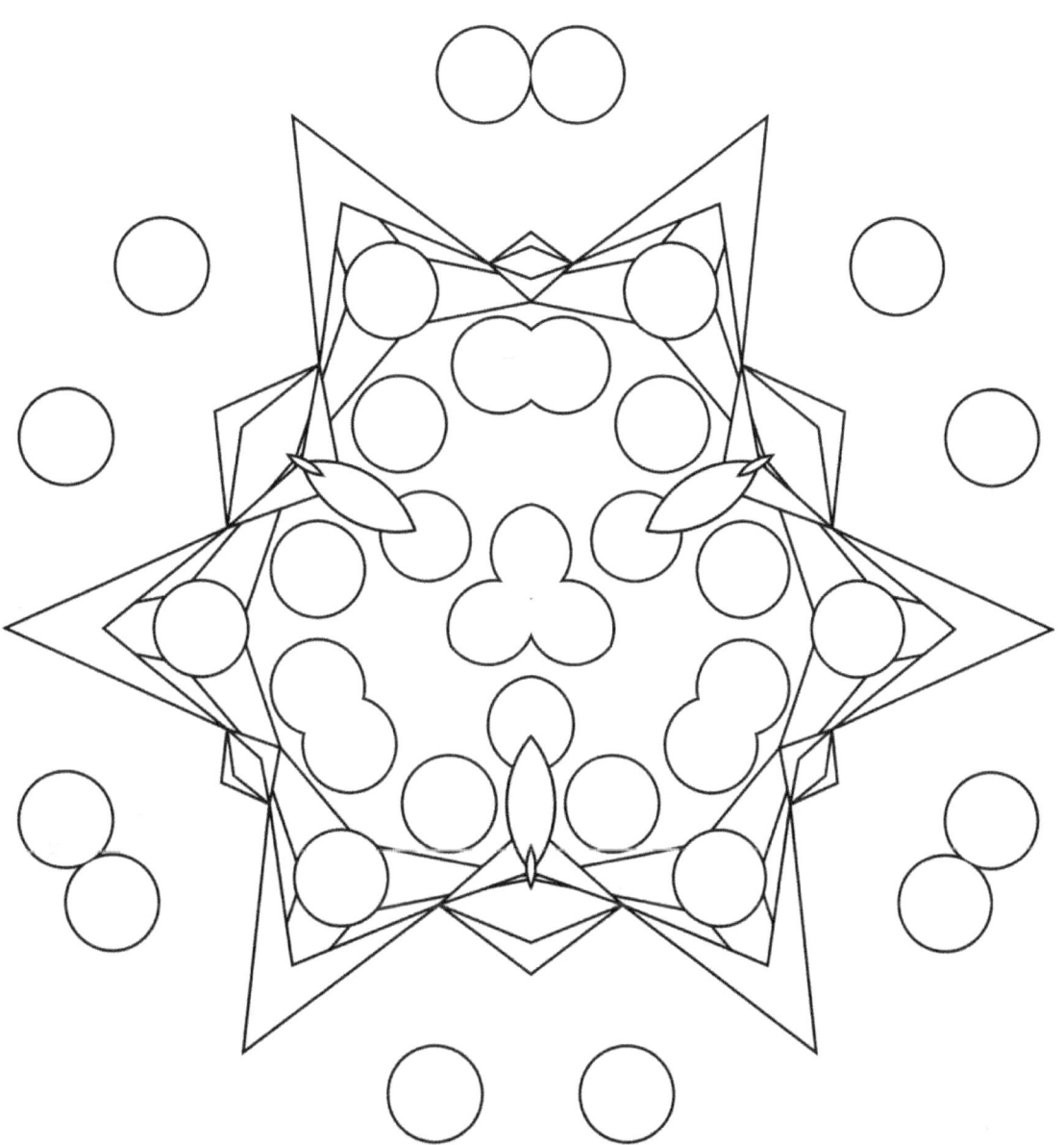

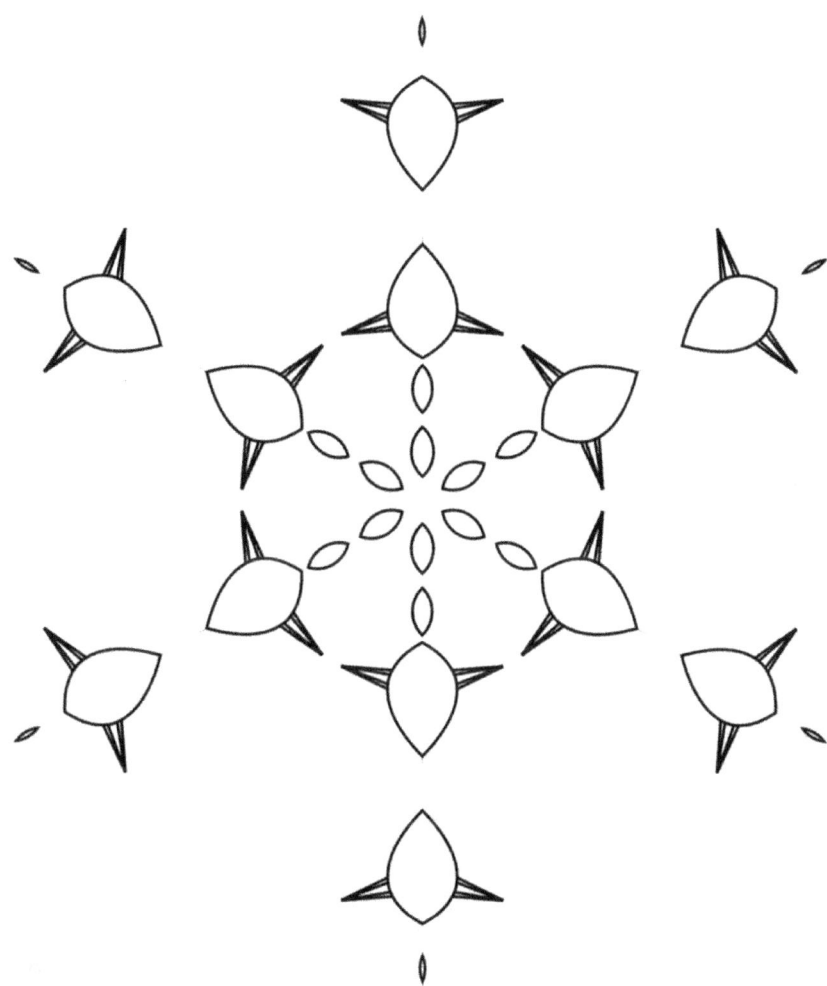

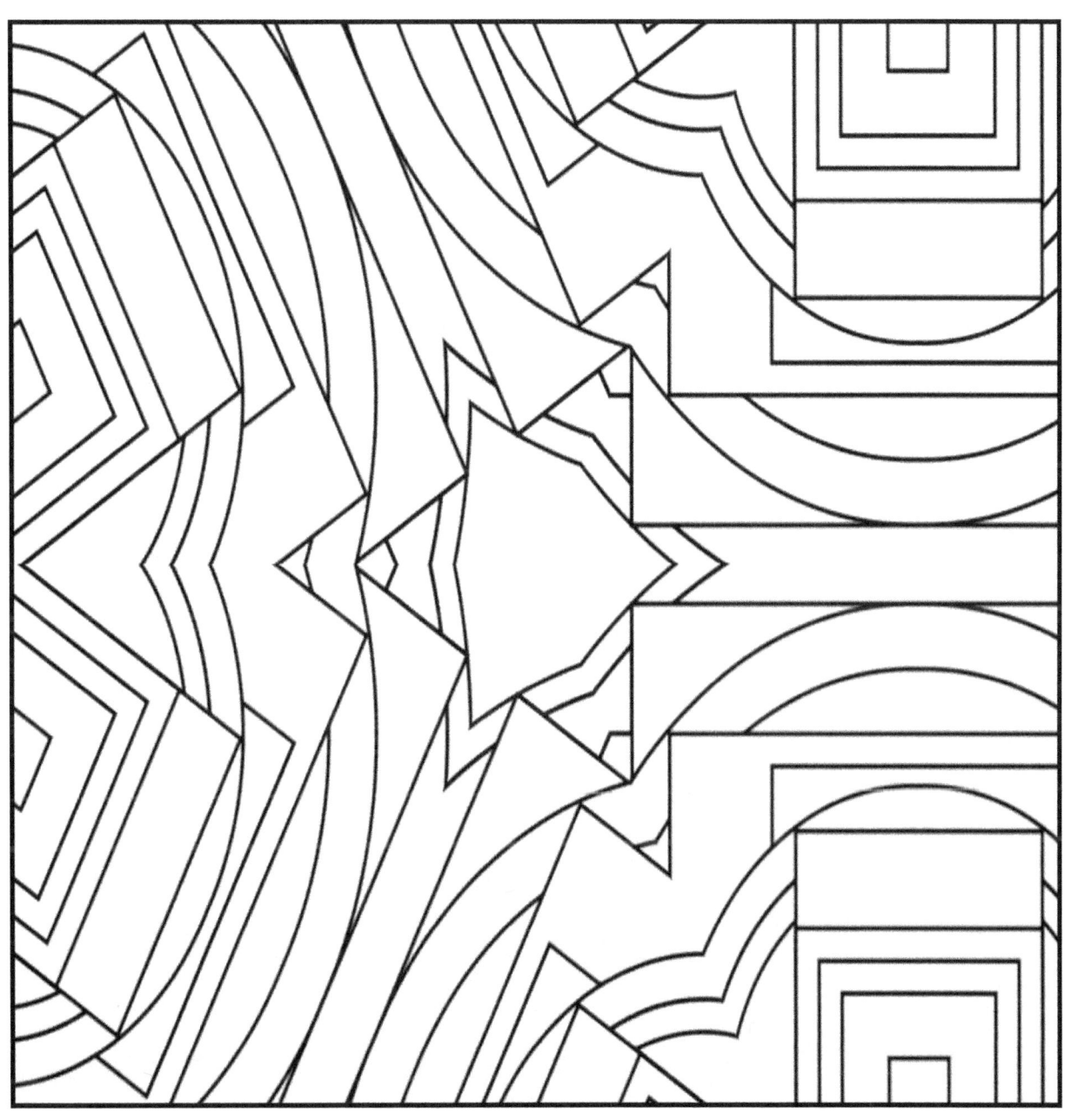

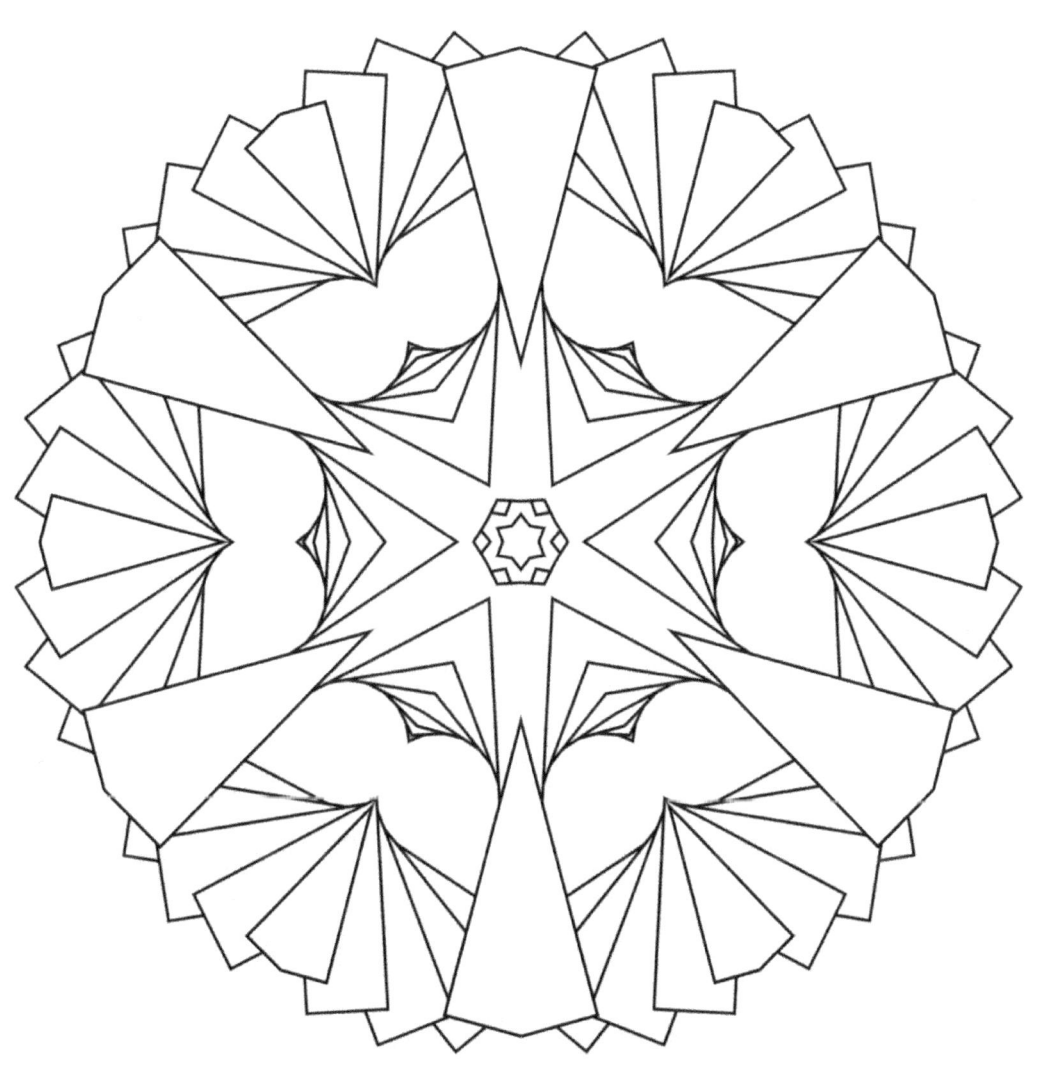

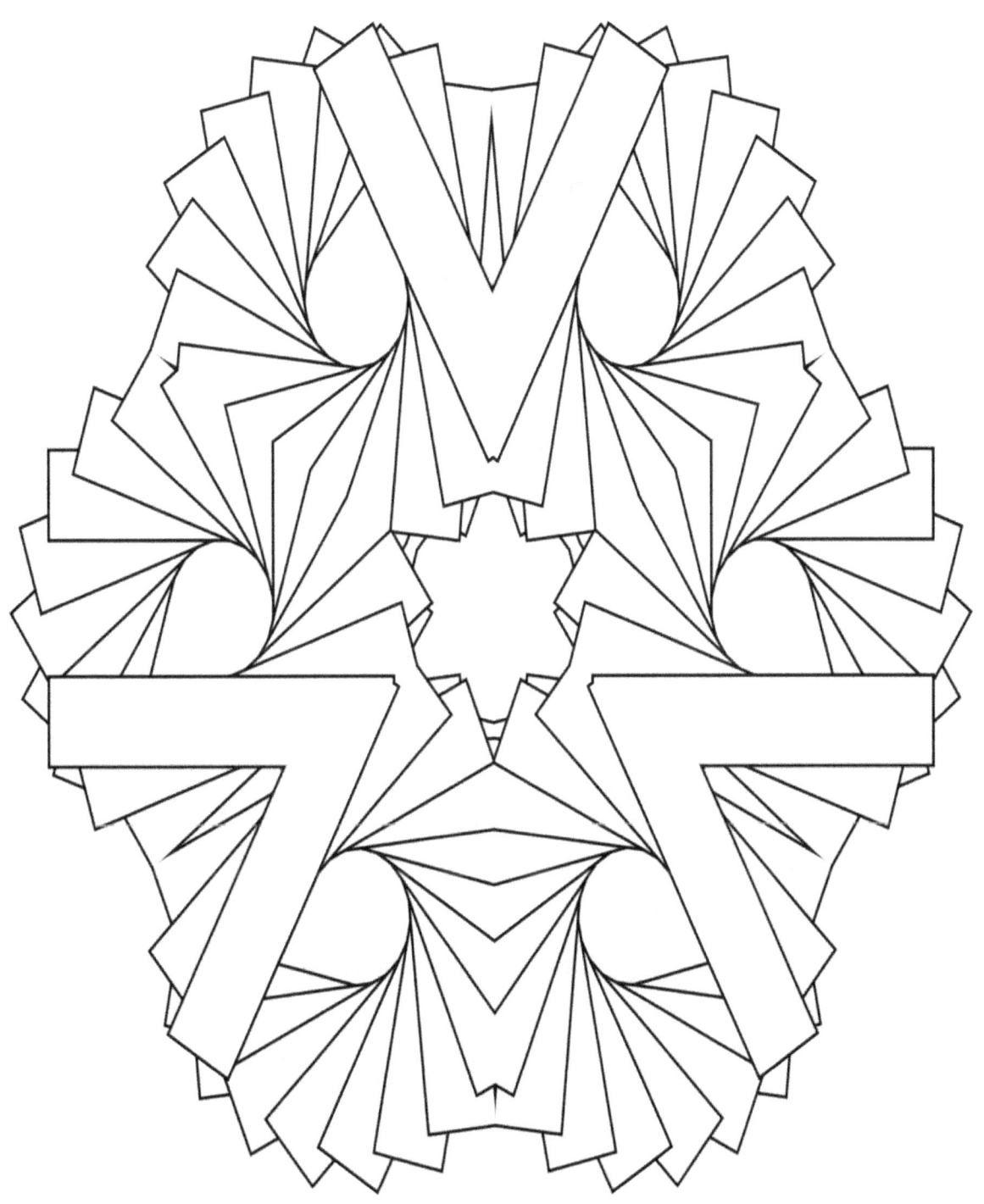

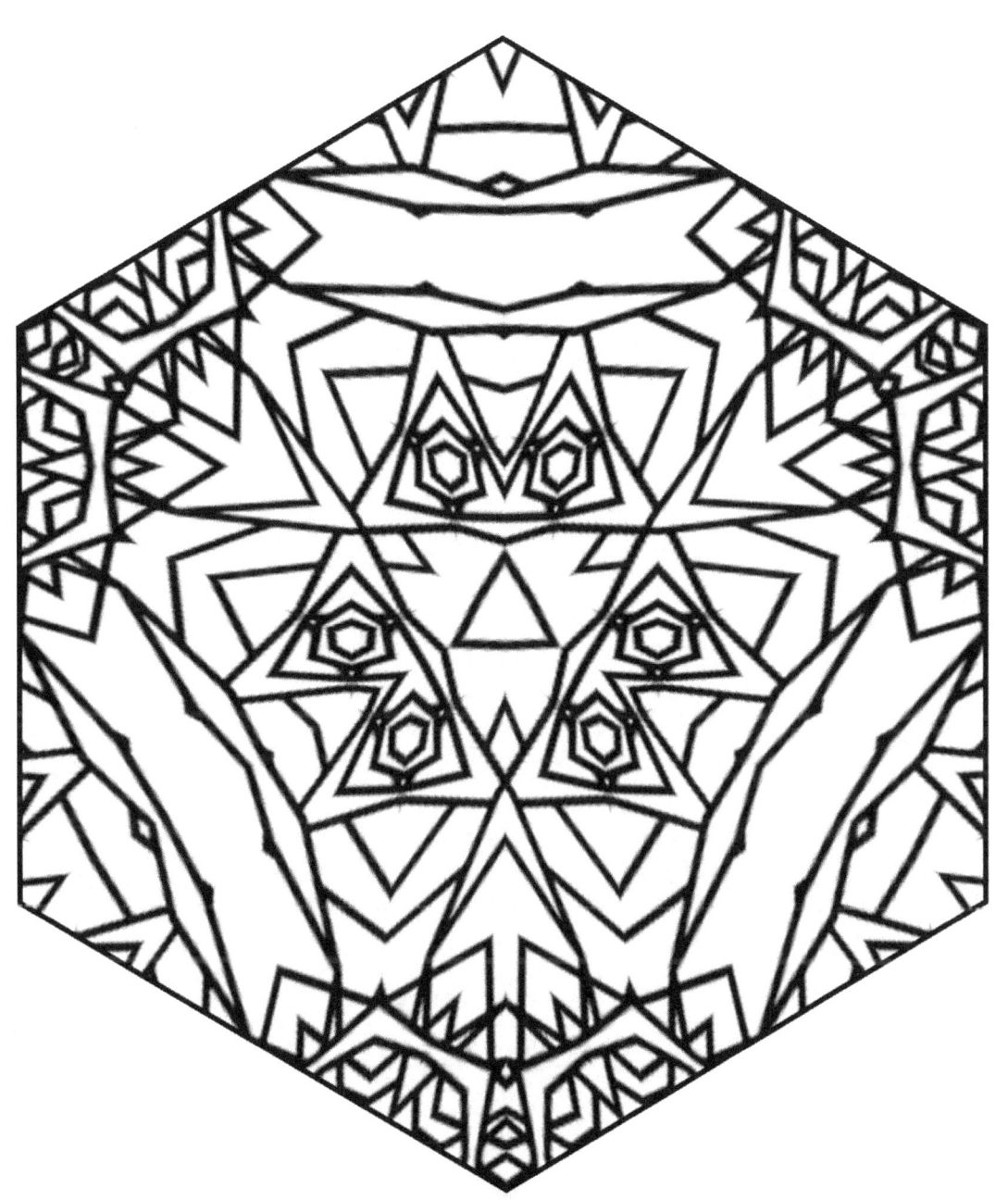

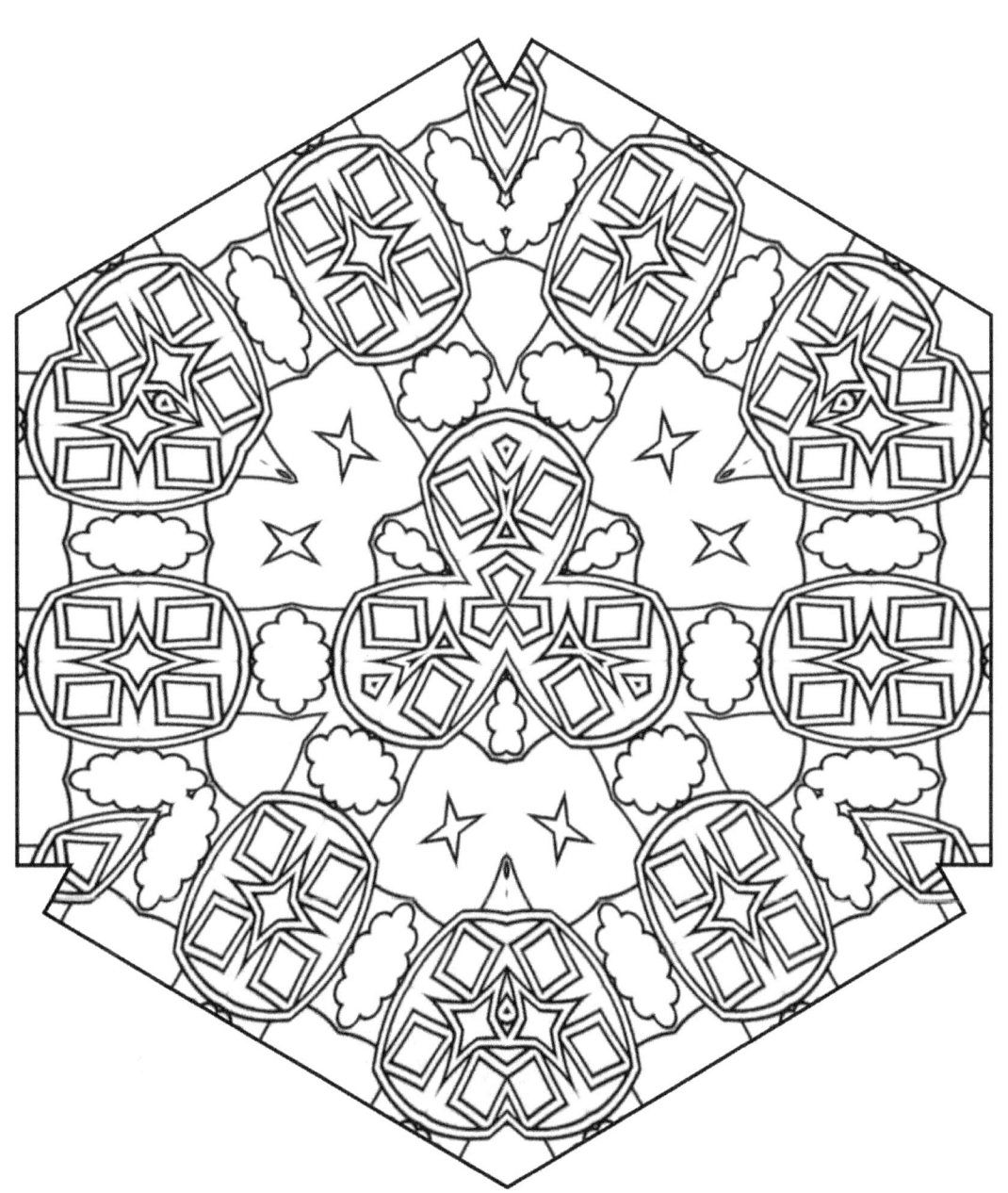

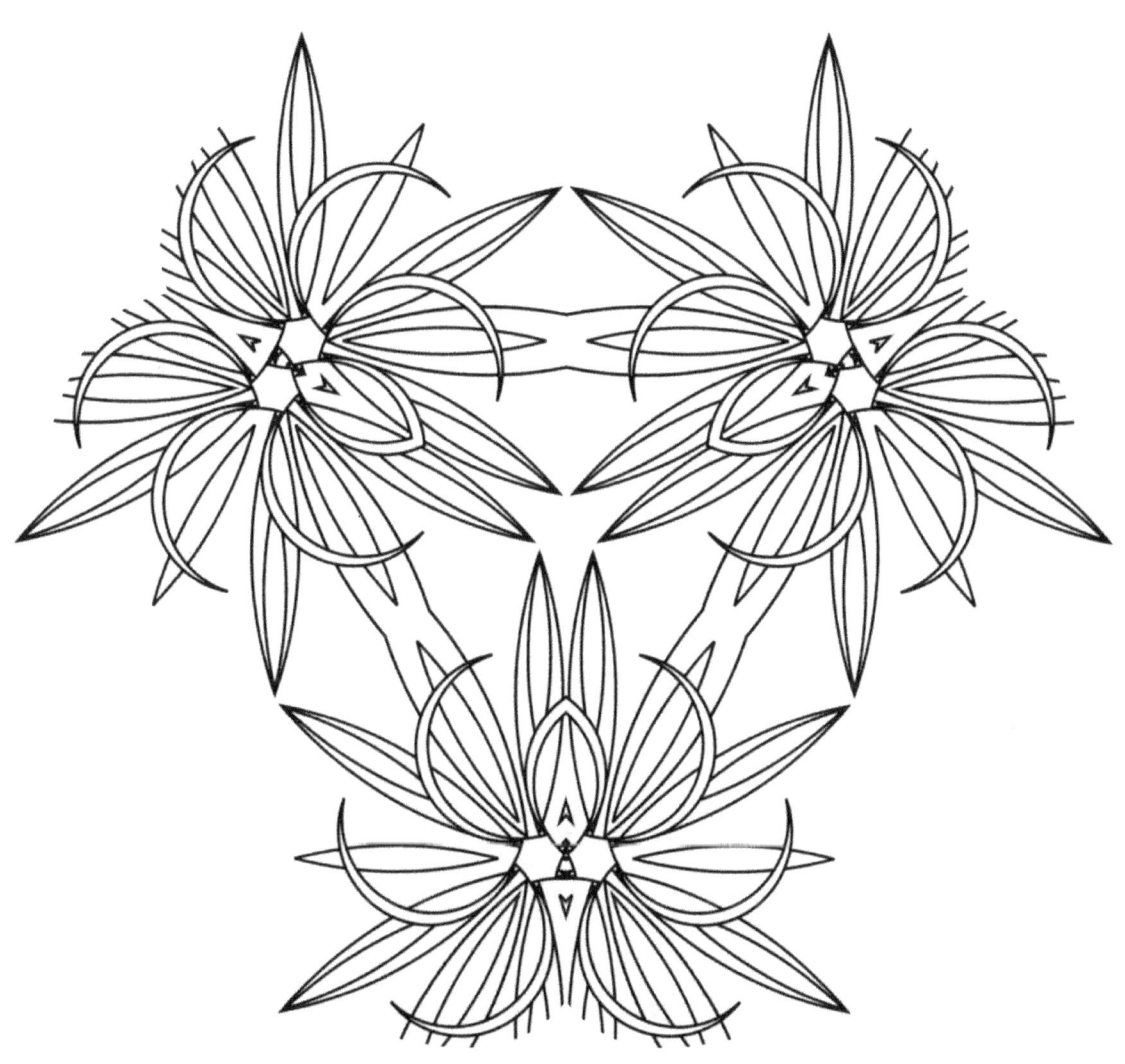

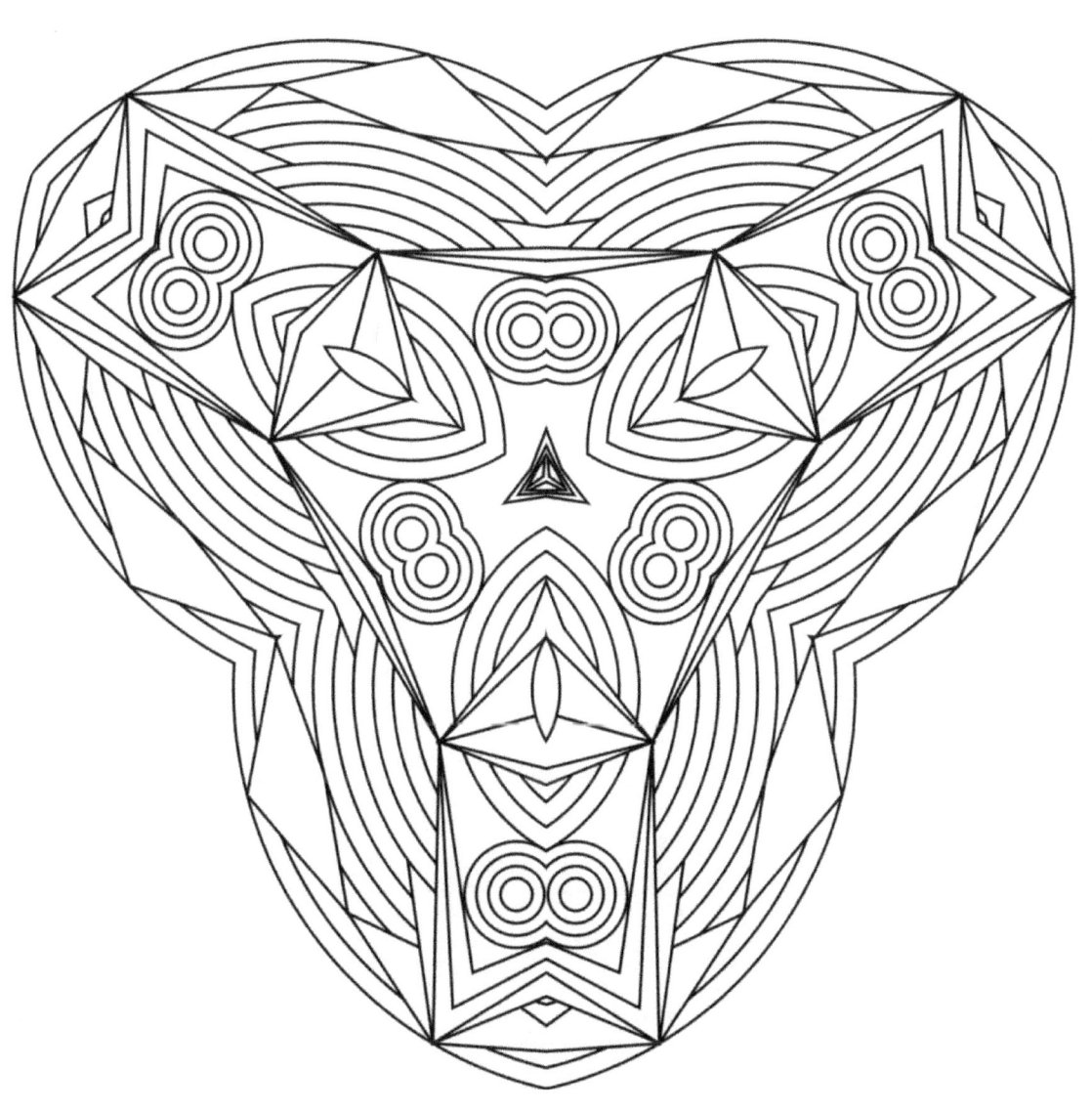

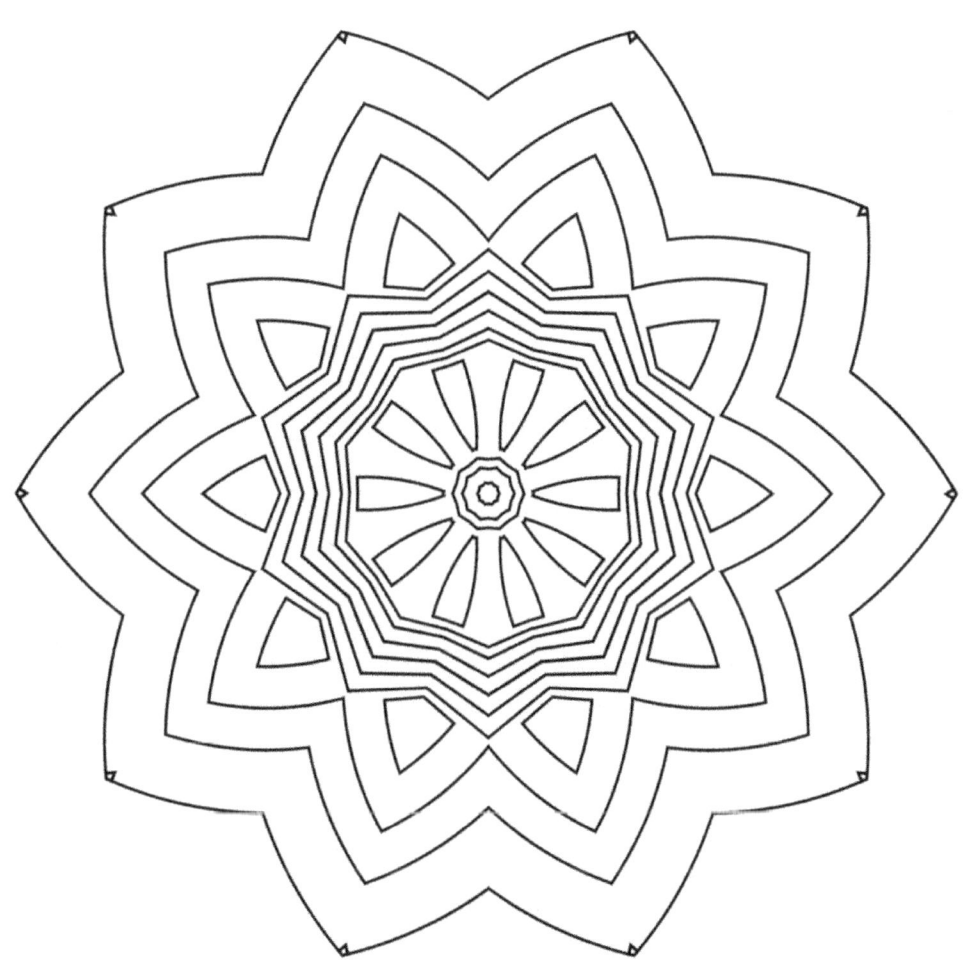

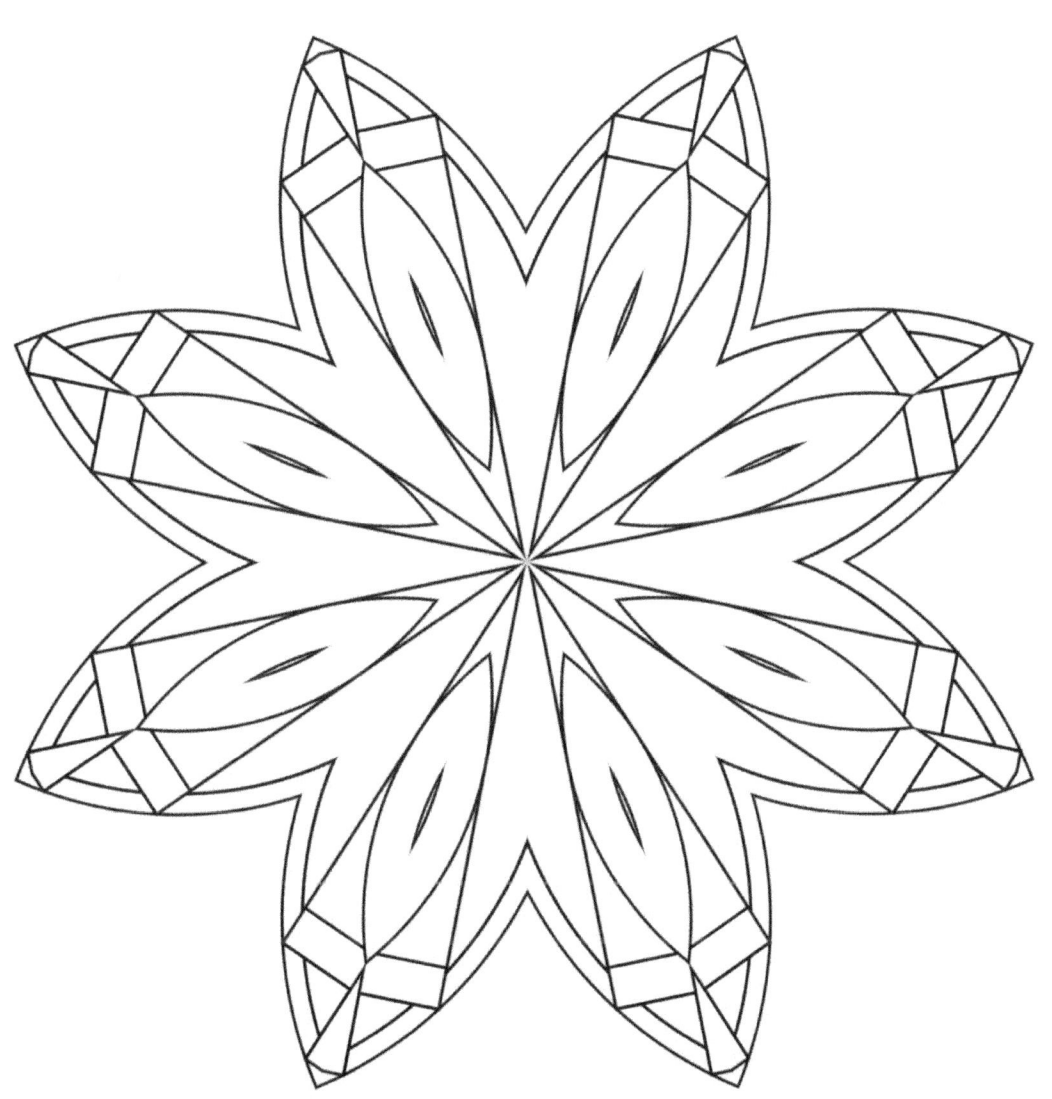

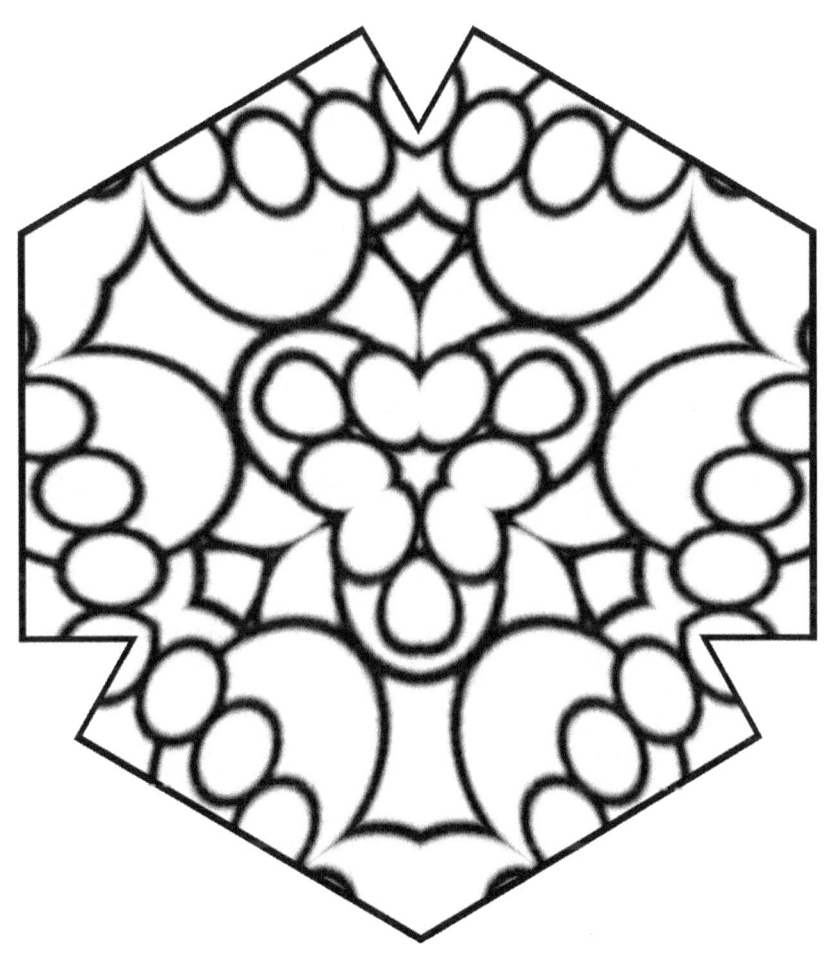

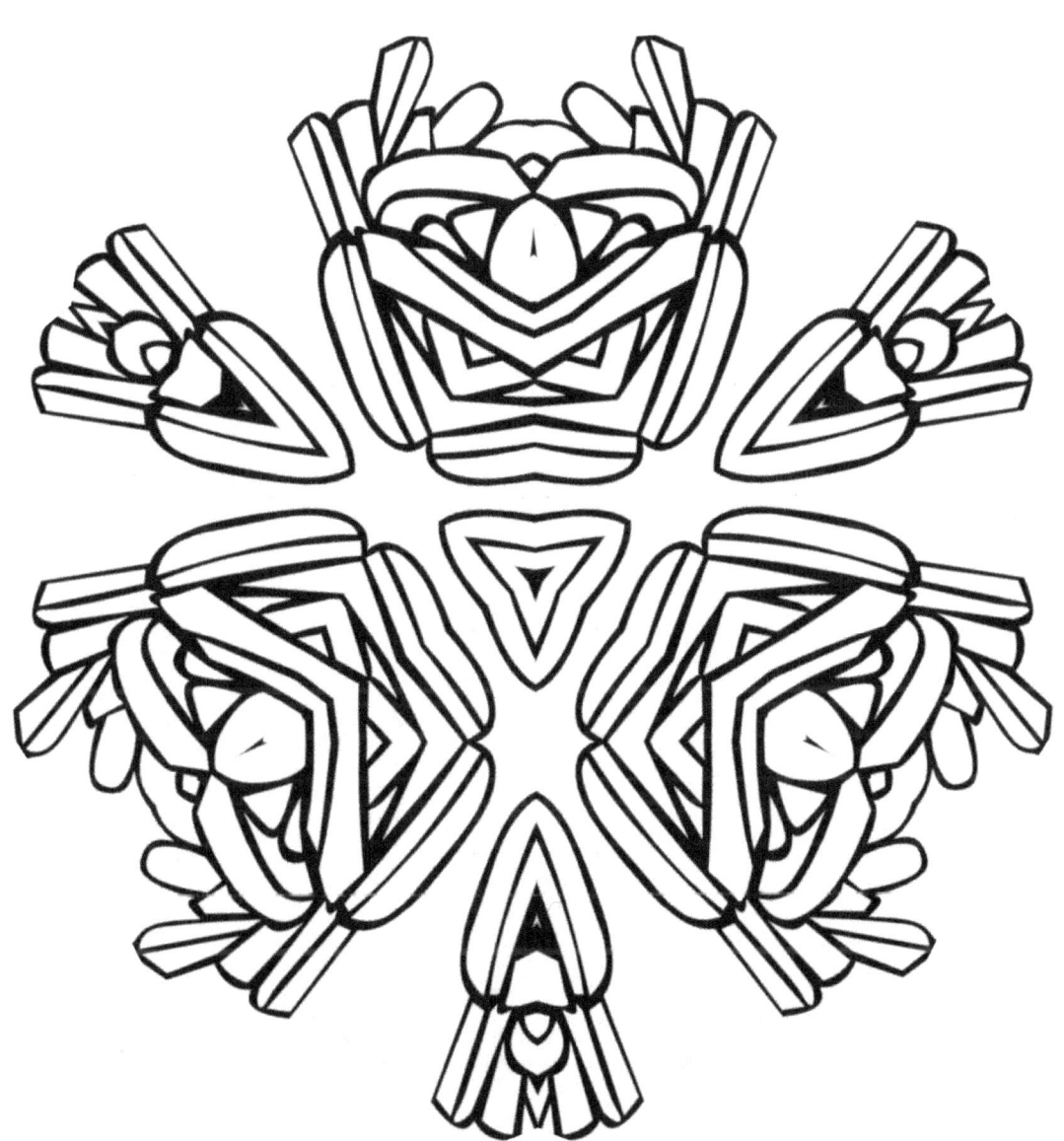

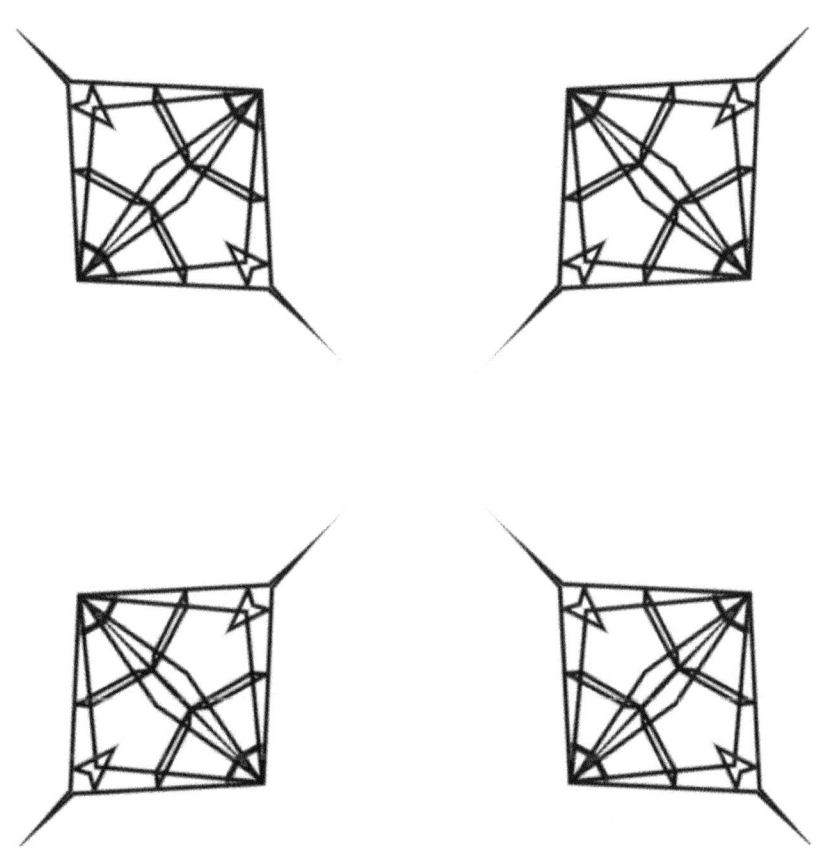

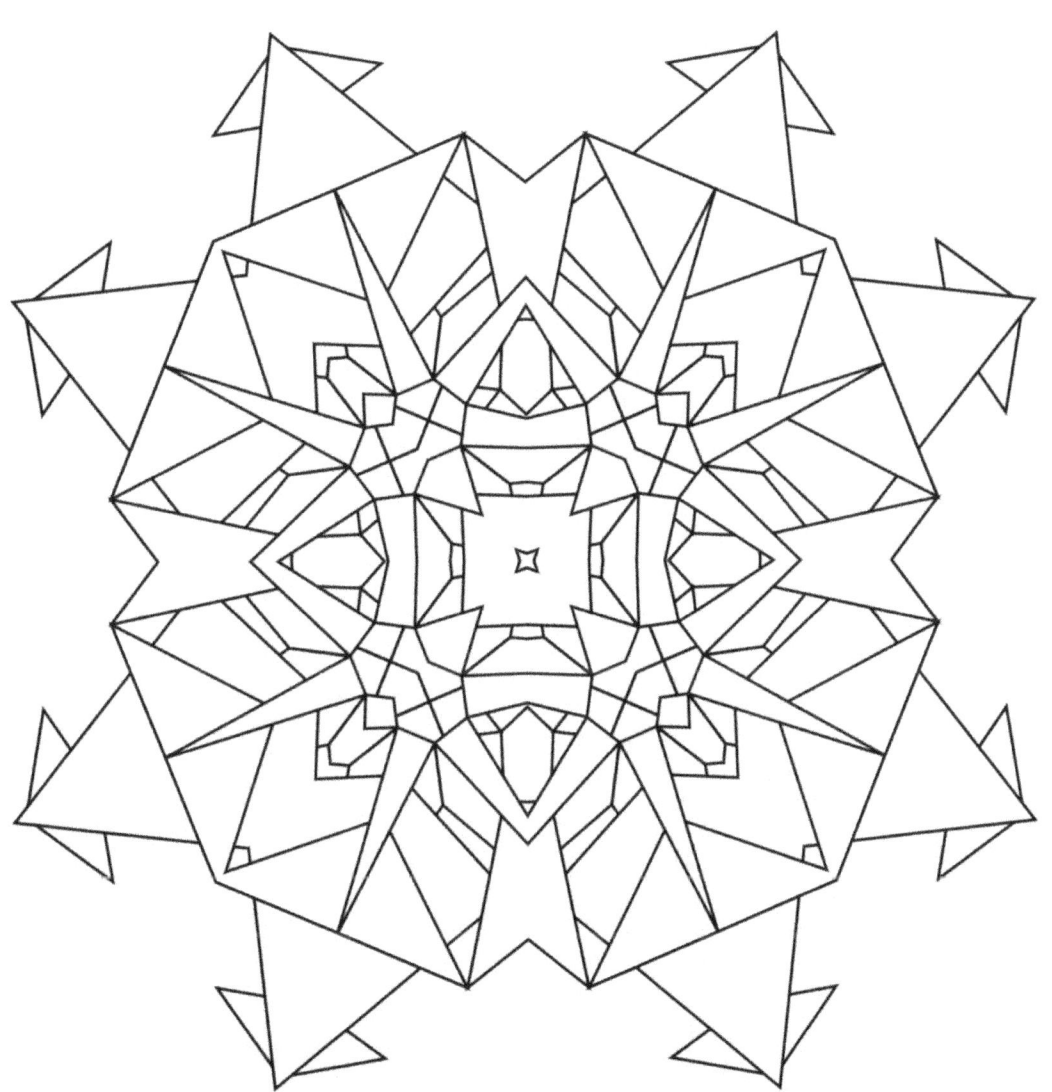

www.ingramcontent.com/pod-product-compliance
Lightning Source LLC
Chambersburg PA
CBHW062159220526
45470CB00009B/2871